Emergency Preparedness Basics

Peace of Mind Through Preparation

A Guide to Successfully Creating Your Emergency Plans

Written by: Eric P. Baird

www.EmPrepBasics.com

Copyright 2012 by EPB Industries
All rights reserved. This book, or parts thereof, may be reproduced with permission only.

For permission write to:
EPB Industries
Attention: Eric P. Baird
2222 Huntington Lane Unit 4
Redondo Beach, CA 90278

Emergency Preparedness Basics
3nd Edition 2012
By Eric Baird

Published by EPB Industries
Redondo Beach, CA USA
www.EmPrepBasics.com

Every effort has been made to supply complete and accurate information in this book. All such information is provided as is. Best effort due diligence has been taken to provide credit where credit is due. All information contained in this book is subject to change without notice.

Dedication

This book is dedicated to emergency responders throughout the world. Men and women, who serve their communities as police officers, fire fighters and community organizers. Your willingness to help those in need is inspiring.

For our reader, I honor and welcome you to a world of emergency preparedness. This book is designed to lighten your burden should catastrophe, earthquake, hurricane, or terrorist attack, put you and your family in harm's way. I hope you will be encouraged as you design your plans for home, work and "on the go" preparedness. May you gain *peace of mind* as you complete this book.

Acknowledgements

I want to thank those who have helped refine this book. It is the result of many contributions, and would not exist without your support. I am very grateful.

Special thanks to:

Betty Rodgers, Debbie Bina O'Brien, Marcelle McCullough, Tawna Sparling, Tracy Hopkins, Glenn Willis, Gary Sessions, Larry Ragel, Paul & Pilar Baird, David & Deena Christensen & family, my amazing wife, Chelise Christensen Baird, and my other creations, Kalem, Paxton & Lucy. Not to mention the countless others who have inspired and shown me the way.

Disclaimer

This guide is for informational purposes only. It is designed to support you in your efforts to increase your safety and survival. Many factors contribute to your safety in an emergency or disaster situation. Take responsibility for your safety and that of your family. It is better to be prepared, than to wish you had done more.

Table of Contents

INTRODUCTION 9
INSTRUCTIONS 10
PREFACE: YOUR EMERGENCY PLANS 17
SECTION I 19
EMERGENCY PREPAREDNESS AT HOME 21
    SAFE SPOTS: 22
    DANGER SPOTS: 22
    EVACUATION ROUTES: 23
    UTILITY SHUT-OFFS: 23
    DUCK, COVER AND HOLD ON: 24
    SPECIFIC PERSONAL ITEMS: 24
    PET PREPARATION: 25
    MEETING PLANS: 27
    SCHOOLS AND DAY-CARE CENTER POLICIES: 28
    GET TO KNOW YOUR NEIGHBORS: 29
    LEARN WHAT CAUSES: 29
    DISCUSS AFTERSHOCKS: 30
    KITCHEN SAFETY: 30
    ASSEMBLE YOUR CHILD'S EMERGENCY KIT: 30
    LIVING WITHOUT ELECTRICITY: 32
    BEHAVIORAL CHANGES: 33
SUPPLY STORAGE 35
    SUPPLY STORAGE: 35
    FOOD STORAGE: 37
EMERGENCY LIGHTING & ELECTRICITY 39
    FLASHLIGHTS: 39
    LIGHT STICKS: 39
    EMERGENCY LIGHTING: 39
    RADIOS: 40
    SPECIAL POWER NEEDS: 40
    CHECKING UTILITIES: 40
EMERGENCY CASH AND IMPORTANT DOCUMENTS 43
    HAVE A CASH STASH: 43
    POCKET CHANGE: 43
    IMPORTANT DOCUMENTS: 43
    STORAGE TIPS: 45
FIRST AID TRAINING AND SUPPLIES 47
    COMMON INJURIES: 47

    FIRST AID COURSES: 47
    FIRST AID KITS: 48

EMERGENCY CAMPING OUT **51**
    OUTDOOR LIVING: 51
    OUTDOOR COOKING: 53
    COOKING SUPPLIES: 53
    SPECIAL TIPS: 54
    FRESHEN UP YOUR WATER AND FOOD SUPPLIES: 54
    WATER STORAGE: 55
    ALTERNATE WATER SOURCES: 56
    FOOD SELECTION AND STORAGE: 56

LEARN NOT TO BURN **59**
    FIRE EXTINGUISHERS: 59
    HOW TO OPERATE: 60
    BUYING TIPS: 61
    SMOKE & CO2 DETECTORS: 61
    SAFETY TIPS: 62

SECTION II **63**

EMERGENCY PREPAREDNESS AT WORK **65**
    TRAVEL TIME, DESTINATION & EVACUATION ROUTE: 66
    SAFE SPOTS: 67
    DANGER SPOTS: 67
    EVACUATION ROUTES: 68
    72 HOUR OFFICE KIT: 68

SECTION III **71**

EMERGENCY PREPAREDNESS "ON THE GO" **73**
    SOCIAL PLANNING: 74
    72 HOUR CAR KIT: 74
    HOTEL & OVERNIGHT STAY: 75
    WHAT TO DO WHILE DRIVING: 77

CONCLUSION **79**

APPENDICES **83**
    ADDITIONAL INTERNET RESOURCES 84
    PREPAREDNESS GIFT LIST 86
    GRAPH PAPER 90
    QUICK REFERENCE CARDS 95
    REMOVABLE CHECKLIST 99
    ABOUT THE AUTHOR 101

Introduction

CONGRATULATIONS! You are now on your way to expanding your understanding of emergency preparedness. The purpose of this book is to guide you as you develop your emergency plans.

Let me reassure you. **You can do this!** As you complete this book, you will get a clearer understanding of what you have and a better idea of what you need. Having a plan in vital. As the saying goes, "where there is no vision the people perish". Let's create that vision of emergency preparedness and gather the supplies you need. With these together you'll have less to worry about and can focus on what matters most, you and your family. My commitment is that you gain **confidence** and **peace of mind** putting one foot in front of the other, as you reach that goal.

Your commitment: (Fill in below)

I, _____ commit to being prepared for any emergency. I will create my emergency plans for home, work, and when I am "on the go", for myself and my family. I will gather the items I need. I will help those I love, live with and work with. I will complete this process by:_____(date).

Signature:_____Date:_____

Instructions

This book will serve as an interactive guide and log book. It will help you as you develop your personal and family plan. Soon you'll have it all together and accessible when you need it.

Now that you have made a commitment to be prepared, let's start by listing all the individuals you're responsible for and would like your plan to include. Remember this plan should have three aspects to think about, (1) home, (2) work, and (3) "on the go". List the names below:

_____   _____
_____   _____
_____   _____
_____   _____
_____   _____

The individuals listed above are your main reason for you to create this plan.

Next you'll have the opportunity to think of other reasons to be prepared. Ask yourself, "Why should I be prepared?" Your answers will provide astonishing power behind your actions. They may be simple ideas like, "I love my family and don't want them to suffer" or "I don't want to rely on the government for support."

Whatever your reasons, make sure it's passionate, because it will drive you to complete this book and become better prepared. Write your reasons below.

Why I Want To Be Prepared:

_____
_____
_____
_____
_____
_____
_____
_____
_____
_____
_____
_____
_____
_____
_____
_____
_____
_____
_____
_____
_____
_____
_____

With your reasons in place, let's get started on creating your plans. This includes evaluating your current preparedness status at home, work and "on the go".

As you progress through this book, you will notice boxes at the beginning of every topic or section that requires you to complete a task. Put a check mark in the box ☑ signifying that you have completed that task. If you come across items you have not yet completed, or need more time to complete, write an anticipated completion date in the margin. It doesn't have to be perfect. You're just drawing a line in the sand setting a goal that needs to be completed.

Also, in the back of the book is a **Removable Checklist**. Carefully cut this page out or download it from our website. Place it somewhere visible so you can see it on a daily basis. A suggestion is on the refrigerator. Fill it in as you progress, checking off completed tasks. With diligence, you will be well on your way to completing your emergency plans.

As an extra bonus near the back of the book is a convenient **Preparedness Gift List**, with price ranges and suggested items you can use as gifts for the people you love for special occasions. The items are very practical and the receiving party will be grateful. Perhaps you could suggest some of the items as gifts to you.

Lastly, please share this book and the information you've learned with family, friends, and neighbors. They will appreciate your concern and will quickly see the value that completing this book will bring.

Good luck with your plans, and be sure to find us online to share your experiences and triumphs as you become emergency prepared.

Thank you,
Eric P. Baird

These pages are for you to create a collage of photos of your family, friends, coworkers, teammates, pets, favorite places, and anything else you love!

Preface: Your Emergency Plans

Have you ever wondered what would happen if an emergency were to occur right now? Where would you go? What would you do? Since emergencies cannot be predicted, it is imperative that you are ready wherever you are. You could be at home sleeping, or at work getting ready to take your lunch break. You could be at the movies or just out doing your grocery shopping. Wherever you are, being prepared will make the difference.

Your emergency plans will be vital in sustaining you in these situations. *Peace of mind* comes from knowing that you are prepared, which includes having what you need and knowing what to do. This guide will help you gain that peace of mind.

Section I

Emergency Preparedness At Home

Chapter One

Emergency Preparedness at Home

Home will require the bulk of your effort, and can be considered your base.

Do you and those you love know the safest spots in your home during an earthquake or other emergency? Have you taken an inventory of places to avoid? Does everyone know where to meet if the family becomes separated? Do they know how to report their physical conditions and whereabouts?

The safety and well-being of your loved ones is important. In this first chapter of creating your home emergency plans, basic questions will be answered. If you have a child or children it is suggested that you do these activities with them. Knowing that your children are prepared will bring greater peace of mind.

Take time now to develop your home emergency plan. If you already have a plan developed, place a copy of it in this book. It doesn't hurt to take the time now to review and update it.

☐ **Safe Spots:**

Using the graph paper provided in the back of this book, draw out all the areas of your home and identify safe spots in each room such as sturdy desks and tables, exterior walls or corners. These will provide protection from falling objects. Draw these in **Green** and put the letter **S (Safe)** in the middle and circle it. You may also list the rooms below and where to go to find protection.

_____

_____

_____

_____

_____

☐ **Danger Spots:**

Using the same graph paper, identify places in each room that pose a danger. Items such as windows, tall unsecured furniture, objects on shelves that could fall, appliances, hanging mirrors, plants, pictures, ceiling lights, and tall brick structures like chimneys both inside or outside the house can cause severe damage during a disaster or emergency. Draw these in **Red** and put the letter **D (Danger)** in the middle and circle it. You may also list the rooms below and the items to stay away from.

_____

_____

_____

_____

_____

☐ **Evacuation Routes:**

Using the same or a different sheet of graph paper, draw out and locate exits and alternate routes to leave your home should an emergency arise. Mark exit routes from each room in **Blue** with arrows marking the path. Also be sure to mark your final outside meeting point with a big **X**. Remember windows may need to become exit routes in case of a fire. Finding the best location to exit a 2nd story window will require a little extra planning. Equipment such as fire extinguishers, rollup ladders and ropes are available online or at your local emergency supply store. Use the spaces below to briefly describe your meeting location and your exit routes.

_____
_____
_____
_____
_____

☐ **Utility Shut-Offs:**

On a new graph page, draw a bird's eye view of your home. Now in **Red** draw potential dangers such as power lines and poles, large trees, a neighbor's gas meter (in case you need to shut it off), and other potentially dangerous items, like fire hydrants, and electrical junction boxes, around your home. Locate your shut-off valves for water, gas and electricity, and draw them in **Red**. Teach mature family members when and how to shut them off. Gas should be turned off only if you smell or find a leak. If possible contact your utility company. Describe the location below of each utility, and include their company contact information.

Water: _____

_____ Phone # _____

Gas: _____

_____ Phone # _____

Electricity: _____

_____ Phone # _____

☐ **Duck, Cover and Hold On:**

If you are indoors when an earthquake strikes, look for something sturdy to duck next to and drop to the floor. Visualize this as you stand in each room or practice this now:

- ☐ Drop to the Floor.
- ☐ Protect your head and neck by covering them with your arms and hands.
- ☐ Hold on to the piece of furniture. If you take cover under it, be ready to move with it.
- ☐ Hold your position until the shaking stops and it is safe to move.

☐ **Specific Personal Items:**

Specific personal items include items such as: special foods, medications (OTC/Rx), eye glasses, life-sustaining equipment, wheelchairs, canes or walkers, and/or strollers. Be sure to store these items in a location that is easy to access.

Plan for family members who have special needs, such as senior citizens, disabled or handicapped, young children, and those who need special medication, or require special treatments. List below the special items you will need to bring and where they are securely kept.

_____
_____
_____
_____
_____

☐ **Pet Preparation:**

Planning for a pet can sometimes be overlooked. Be sure to plan for your pet appropriately. The following will help prepare your pet in case of an emergency.

- ☐ Make sure you pet is licensed and registered. Include their information with your important documents.
- ☐ Have your pet's name and license number securely tagged to their collar or use an RFID microchip.
- ☐ Have a picture of your pet.
- ☐ Develop a plan with a friend or neighbor, who can care for your pet in case you are at work or unable to get home within 24 hours. Provide them a written authority to act on your behalf for the care of your pet. The person who will take care of my pet in an emergency is: _____
  _____ Phone #: _____
- ☐ Make sure your pet's vaccinations are current.

- Make or purchase a Pet Kit with your pet's favorite supplies. Items should include:
  - Food & Water
  - Bowls
  - Cleaning supplies, trash bags
  - Extra Collar and leash
  - First Aid Kit
  - Pet medications
  - Disposable litter box
  - Cat Litter
  - Transportation Crate
- Store your pet's go bag with your other emergency supplies. Be sure to label it if you have multiple pets.
- Keep your cool. Your pet will respond to your level of anxiety and may hide or become difficult to handle.
- Keep your pet calm. Pay close attention to your pet's behavior. Recognize that your pet may become timid and fearful just before, during and after a major event, and remain that way for some time.
- If you lose your pet, check with the local animal shelter. My local animal shelter and phone number is:
  - Animal Shelter: _____
    _____
  - Contact: _____
  - Phone #: _____

☐ My Pets and their Names: _____

_____

_____

☐ Meeting Plans:

It is important that family members know where and how to reunite after a disaster or emergency. Knowing everyone is alive and well will help family members cope with the situation more easily.

Include the following in your family emergency plan:

☐ Near Home Meeting place or places:

_____

_____

_____

☐ Out-of-state contacts:

Name: _____

Address: _____

_____ Phone #: _____

Name: _____

Address: _____

_____ Phone #: _____

Name: _____

Address: _____

_____ Phone #: _____

It might be easier for these contacts to reach you so ask them to contact you after 24 hours if they are aware of an emergency and don't hear from you within that time frame. Phone lines might not reach out but sometimes calls will be able to get in.

☐ **Schools and Day-Care Center Policies:**
Be sure to check with your school for its policies on reuniting children with their parents.

- ☐ Get a copy of the school's emergency plan.
- ☐ Emergency shelter, kids will be located at if different than the school: _____

- ☐ How will you get there? Reassure your child that you will do everything possible to reunite with them. _____

- ☐ What you expect of your child/ren while in the schools custody? Be sure they know your expectations are for their behavior. _____

- ☐ Designate someone to pick up your child/ren if you think you won't be unable to within 24 hours after an emergency. We designate:
  Name:_____Phone #_____
  to retrieve our child/ren in case of emergency.

☐ **Get To Know Your Neighbors:**
Get to know your neighbors! On the spaces provided below list the names of your three nearest neighbors and their phone numbers. Share what you're up to and let them know you're willing to help them.

☐ Name: _____
　 Address: _____
　 _____ Phone #: ____
☐ Name: _____
　 Address: _____
　 _____ Phone #: ____
☐ Name: _____
　 Address: _____
　 _____ Phone #: ____

Your family will have many details to attend to, and so will your neighbors. Develop a plan that covers potential problems. Share the responsibilities with everyone based on their probable location. It may be difficult to travel as a result of the damage to roads and infrastructure. So work with neighbors and plan ahead!

☐ **Learn What Causes:**

　☐ **Earthquakes:** Explain why the ground and buildings shake. Remind everyone that the shaking will stop. Research your area and explain why earthquakes occur.

Let your child/ren ask questions and discover the answers together. Learn the difference between fact and fiction.

_____
_____
_____

☐ **Hurricanes:** What causes major storms?_____

_____
_____
_____

☐ **Discuss Aftershocks:**
    ☐ Ensure everyone understands that aftershocks are normal
    ☐ Plan where you will take cover when they occur.

☐ **Kitchen Safety:**
    ☐ Anchor heavy appliances and furniture
    ☐ Install latches on cupboard doors
    ☐ Store food and water in multiple secure locations

☐ **Assemble Your Child's Emergency Kit:**

Help your child/ren assemble their emergency kit. Kit's should be to their liking and meet their needs. Include the following special items:

    ☐ Identification (Quick Reference Card)
    ☐ Contact information
    ☐ A note from parents or guardians
    ☐ Special pictures of family, friends or pets
    ☐ A special toy such as a book or stuffed animal

Children's Kits should include the following:
- ☐ Food and Water:
    - ☐ 6 juice boxes or water bottles/boxes
    - ☐ 12 calorie rich food bars, like breakfast bars
    - ☐ Favorite snacks or candy
    - ☐ Water Purification Tablets
- ☐ Light and Communication:
    - ☐ Flashlight with extra batteries.
    - ☐ Survival Whistle
- ☐ 3 Green Emergency Glow Sticks
- ☐ Shelter and Warmth:
    - ☐ Warm coat and gloves, climate appropriate
    - ☐ Polar fleece blanket
    - ☐ Emergency poncho
    - ☐ Hand and body warming heat pads, (air activated)
    - ☐ Respiratory dust mask,(look for N95 rating)
- ☐ Hygiene Kit Include:
    - ☐ Soap & shampoo
    - ☐ Toothbrush & toothpaste
    - ☐ Toilet paper & wet wipes
    - ☐ 2-3 Pocket Tissue Packs
    - ☐ Female pads as needed (also good for cuts)
- ☐ 45 Piece First Aid Kit
    - ☐ 10 spot bandages
    - ☐ 10 sheer junior bandages
    - ☐ 5 sheer medium bandages

- ☐ 5 sheer strip bandages
- ☐ 3 clear strip bandages
- ☐ 2 antibacterial wipes
- ☐ 2 alcohol pads
- ☐ 2 antiseptic packs
- ☐ 2 gauze pads
- ☐ 2 fabric strip bandages
- ☐ 1 extra-large fabric strip bandage
- ☐ 1 triangular bandages
- ☐ Entertainment may include:
  - ☐ Activity books, coloring books & crayons, origami, etc, keeping their minds occupied
  - ☐ Children's toys such as jump rope, paddle ball, toy cars or play figures
  - ☐ Playing cards, like Uno or Phase 10. Many games could be played with a regular deck of cards

Visit www.EmPrepBasics.com for preassembled kits and more! Or visit your local emergency preparedness store for added help.

☐ Living Without Electricity:

Enjoy an entire evening without using electricity. Prepare everyone, especially youngsters, for the possibility of power outages. Have fun with it! Go out for a "flashlight" walk around the block. Have a "flashlight" dinner. Be creative and develop your own idea of things to do together. Tell stories instead of watching television. Use extreme caution if you decide to use candles. They may fall over if shaken.

☐ **Behavioral Changes:**

After a disaster or major emergency, monitor family members, particularly children, for behavioral changes. Dramatic events can leave people emotionally in shock. Depression is common after earthquakes and can affect up to 72% of those affected. Watch for signs of depression and counter them by speaking positively about the situation, singing songs, reviewing photos and memories of fun times together. Look forward toward a brighter future, by doing work together and finding things to keep them occupied.

Chapter Two

Supply Storage

Having supplies is vital, but where you keep them is equally important! They won't help much if you can't access them. Flashlights, portable radios, first aid kits and other emergency supplies are essential after earthquakes and other disasters, but only if you can retrieve them. Consider the following storage options presented below. However, these are only suggestions. Review your home for the best location and prepare your family. Use discretion and common sense in your preparations.

☐ **Supply Storage:**
Store your emergency supplies in a location that is easily accessible. There are several options for storing emergency supplies, including:

- Backpacks
- Duffel bags
- Heavy plastic trash cans w/ wheels
- Other sealable containers

One of the most important considerations in storing your supplies is determining a location that will be easy to access after a natural or manmade disaster. It is recommended that you **store items in** at least **two separate locations**, in case one is not accessible after an event.

Identify the safe spots in your home as you did when you developed your family emergency plan. Then, determine the locations where you spend the most time and where you will have easy access. Your options may include storing supplies in the following locations:

- Under your bed
- Hallway closet
- Pantry, for use while you are at home
- Backyard, side yard, patio or under a deck
- In 5 gallon buckets out of site behind furniture
- Backpacks, easily carried and stored in multiple locations

You might also consider storing the following supplies in several locations, both inside and outside:

Supply	Location
Flashlights	By your bed, pantry & closet
Sturdy shoes	By your bed
Portable radio	In your getaway bag
Eye glasses	By your bed
Canes, walkers, etc.	By your bed
Adjustable wrench	By the gas meter
Food and water	Pantry, garage or side yard

☐ **Food Storage:**
Remember that storing food and water requires special consideration. Opened packages of sugar, flour, dried fruits and nuts should be stored into screw-top plastic jars or air-tight containers to avoid problems with insects and rodents.

- ☐ Food and water stored in the pantry should be placed on lower shelves to prevent damage to the containers during an earthquake. Shacking can cause things to be jostled around

- ☐ Store your food and water in a dark, cool place to increase their shelf life.

Planning food storage for a family is a large undertaking and can quickly become expensive. We suggest starting a little at a time. Every time you visit the grocery store, buy a few extra cans of food that can be added to your growing storage supply. Before you know it you will have a few weeks worth of food. Research local canneries and find out if they offer larger supplies of canned goods, like flower, pasta, rice, dried fruit and much, much more!

More information regarding food storage and planning is available on the internet. Visit www.EmPrepBasics.com for our favorite places to purchase or make your own food storage supplies.

Chapter Three

Emergency Lighting & Electricity

Every home should have emergency flashlights and spare batteries. Don't be left in the dark when the next emergency strikes. Protect your family by obtaining battery operated flashlights and extra batteries for your home, office and car.

☐ **Flashlights:**
Flashlights can provide psychological comfort and immediate emergency lighting when disasters or other power disruptions occur. However, they are only good when you can find them and know they function properly. It might be a good idea to place a flashlight in every room. This will help children to stay calm, and reassured. Place them in a well know yet secure place. Also maintain an ample supply of batteries, and be sure to check them often, recommended every six months.

☐ **Light Sticks:**
Light sticks are also an excellent source of emergency light and do not require electricity or batteries to operate. Maintain an ample supply for each family member. Shelf life is typically three years.

☐ **Emergency Lighting:**
Emergency lighting can be attached to walls or plugged into electrical sockets along hallways, by doors and in rooms. They activate when electricity is disrupted. They provide a short term solution for sufficient lighting during power outages.

☐ **Radios:**
Reliable information and instructions are essential after a damaging disaster or emergency. Protect yourself and your family by including battery-operated portable radios or televisions and extra batteries in your emergency preparedness kits.

☐ **Special Power Needs:**
Prepare now by including the following items, as appropriate, in your emergency kits: Back-up power, extra batteries for hearing aids other hearing assistance devices, wheelchairs, other medical devices, and whatever else you might need.

☐ **Checking Utilities:**
Disasters can also damage utility lines and appliances, putting your home at risk of fire, and gas inhalation. If you smell gas evacuate your home. Locate your gas meter outside and shut it off.

Before the next emergency:
- ☐ Show responsible family members the location of your electrical service panel and teach them how to turn off service.
- ☐ Conduct family drills and simulate turning off electricity to test family skills.

After an emergency:
- ☐ Determine if electricity is out in your home only or throughout the entire neighborhood.

- ☐ Check for damaged appliances, as well as fallen, loose or damaged electrical wires.
- ☐ Disconnect damaged appliances.
- ☐ Stop power flow at the service panel if your wiring is damaged.
- ☐ Reenergize circuits and bring power back into your home by turning on the main panel first and then each breaker individually.

Safety Tip: Do not use candles, hurricane lamps, lanterns and other objects that rely on an open flame for lighting. Large and even moderate aftershocks that usually accompany damaging earthquakes can topple these items and cause a fire. Items with open flames can also trigger explosions by igniting leaking gas. Be careful before you choose this option.

Chapter Four

Emergency Cash and Important Documents

☐ **Have A Cash Stash:**
A disaster may disrupt power. If this should happen, it won't be "business as usual". Banks and ATM's will be closed for an indefinite period, so your money in the bank may not be available. Your emergency kit should include a sufficient amount of cash to get you through the emergency period. You will need cash to purchase food, gas, and other emergency supplies. Small bills of ones, fives and tens, are best.

☐ **Pocket Change:**
Be sure you also include plenty of change to call out-of-state contacts from a public phone if available in your area (public phone lines are among the first to be restored following a disaster). You can also use a calling card or cell phone with a text message.

☐ **Important Documents:**
You'll also need insurance policies, birth certificates and other vital records after a damaging disaster. Take steps now to protect them. The section below provides an example of documents you should have and suggestions on how to safely store them.

After a damaging disaster or emergency, you will need vital personal documents and information for insurance claims and other matters. Keep the following items and documents in a safe place.

Vital documents to have:

- ☐ Social security cards
- ☐ Birth certificates
- ☐ Marriage and death records
- ☐ Driver's license
- ☐ Wills
- ☐ Deeds
- ☐ Health history, prescriptions, allergies, blood types
- ☐ Recent photos of family members for ID purposes
- ☐ Insurance policies
- ☐ Stocks and bonds
- ☐ Mortgage or rental receipts
- ☐ Employment paycheck stubs
- ☐ Credit cards
- ☐ Recent income tax returns
- ☐ Savings and checking account numbers and books
- ☐ Documentation of valuables*
    - ☐ Computers
    - ☐ Stereo systems
    - ☐ Televisions
    - ☐ Jewelry
    - ☐ Cars
    - ☐ Cameras

*Video or photo documentation will facilitate insurance claims.

☐ **Storage Tips:**
Several options for safely storing important documents, cash and valuables include the following:

- Fireproof Storage Box
- Freezer (Make sure you tightly seal document in a freezer bag before placing them in the freezer)
- The home of your out-of-state contact (send only copies of documents, not the originals)
- Buried in a hermetically sealed container or box.
- Do not use a safe deposit box at a bank, most likely they will be closed and inaccessible.

Chapter Five

First Aid Training and Supplies

You might be on your own for 72 hours or more! During a disaster, people are likely to be injured. Will you be ready to offer first aid? Most likely, you will have to depend on yourself to treat personal injuries, injured family members, friends or coworkers. Outside assistance, including 9-1-1 service will not be available immediately. If you do not have a first aid kit, now is the time to buy or assemble one yourself.

☐ Common Injuries:
Earthquakes can cause a number of injuries. The most common injuries and effects include:
- Lacerations which cause bleeding
- Broken bones, crushed limbs
- Concussion
- Burns
- Cuts from flying/broken glass and falling debris
- Stopped breathing, no heartbeat or no vital signs

☐ First Aid Courses:
If you don't know how to administer first aid including CPR, enroll in a first aid and CPR class today! Courses for adults and children are available through organizations such as local chapters of the American Red Cross, Community Emergency Response Training (CERT), local hospitals and community centers. Sign up!

☐ **First Aid Kits:**
Make sure you have everything you need to treat injuries that occur during a disaster. Assemble and store an emergency first aid kit that includes:

- ☐ First aid book
- ☐ Bandages
- ☐ Adhesive tape
- ☐ Butterfly bandages
- ☐ 3" elastic bandages
- ☐ Roller bandages in multiple sizes
- ☐ Dust masks
- ☐ 4x4 sterile gauze dressings (individually wrapped)
- ☐ Magnifying glass to see splinters
- ☐ Non-allergenic adhesive tape
- ☐ Safety pins
- ☐ Scissors
- ☐ Triangular bandages
- ☐ Antiseptic wipes
- ☐ Blunt-tipped scissors
- ☐ Latex gloves
- ☐ Eye cup or small plastic cup to wash out eyes
- ☐ Emergency (foil) blanket
- ☐ Thermometer
- ☐ Antibiotic salve
- ☐ Tweezers

- ☐ High-absorbency pads
- ☐ Wound disinfectant
- ☐ Saline for eye irrigation
- ☐ Small paper cups
- ☐ Aspirin or acetaminophen
- ☐ Liquid soap
- ☐ Tissues
- ☐ Cold compress
- ☐ Smelling salts

A good suggestion would be to learn what items are in your first aid kit so that you'll be ready to use them. Many of these items can be found at home and can be easily gathered and placed in your kit. Whatever's missing can be purchased locally. Keep your first aid kit close to your other emergency supplies.

You can purchase preassembled first aid kits online by visiting www.EmPrepBasics.com or from your local Emergency Preparedness store.

Chapter Six

Emergency Camping Out

Being prepared means knowing you might have to take living indoors to camping outdoors. This includes your kitchen, bathroom, shower, and sleeping arrangements!

A strong earthquake, flood, wild fire, or other disaster could severely damage or impair utility systems, including gas lines, for long periods, forcing you to live and cook outdoors for days.

Prepare now by including outdoor cooking and camping supplies as part of your emergency kit. Tips on preparing to live and cook outdoors are featured below.

☐ **Outdoor Living:**
Be sure to have the following supplies available so you and your family are prepared to live outdoors if an earthquake or another emergency severely damages your home or utility service is interrupted:

- ☐ Essentials:
    - ☐ Battery operated or self crank radios and flashlights
    - ☐ Blankets, sleeping bags
    - ☐ Canopy or tarp
    - ☐ Warm clothing, coats, pants, sweaters, gloves
    - ☐ Rain gear, umbrella, poncho
    - ☐ Sturdy shoes, boots and socks

- ☐ Essential medications Rx & OTC
- ☐ First Aid book and kits
- ☐ Food (non-perishable)
- ☐ Local maps
- ☐ Rope, tape and trash bags
- ☐ Shovel, hammer and ax
- ☐ Tent(s)
- ☐ Water Filter, Water Storage

☐ Personal Hygiene:
- ☐ Toothbrushes & toothpaste
- ☐ Mouthwash
- ☐ Deodorant
- ☐ Portable shower
- ☐ Soap
- ☐ Washcloths
- ☐ Towelettes (baby wipes)
- ☐ Toilet paper
- ☐ Portable toilet or bucket
- ☐ Plastic trash bags
- ☐ Sunscreen
- ☐ Baking soda to absorb odors

☐ Psychological comfort:
- ☐ Candy
- ☐ Cards
- ☐ Family photos
- ☐ Games

☐ **Outdoor Cooking:**

If an emergency disrupts utility services and forces you to cook outdoors, you can use a camp stove or charcoal grill, but remember: use these items for cooking if you are outdoors only. If necessary, you can also use candle warmers and Sterno canned fuel to heat your food. Canned food can be heated in the can, but you must remove the paper and the lid first to let steam escape. Chafing dishes and fondue pots also can be used as containers. RV stoves make great cooking options if you have one.

☐ **Cooking Supplies:**

Be sure to store at least enough of the cooking supplies to last a few weeks. Choose the supplies for cooking that best suit your family's needs. A list of options follows:

    ☐ Essential Supplies:
- ☐ Barbecue or other outdoor grill
- ☐ Camp stove
- ☐ Dutch ovens of various sizes
- ☐ Sterno-type fuel
- ☐ Charcoal and lighter fluid
- ☐ Propane

Check local laws regarding the use of these products.

    ☐ Eating Supplies
- ☐ Plates (disposable if you prefer)
- ☐ Cups
- ☐ Utensils
- ☐ Paper towels

- ☐ Pots, pans
- ☐ Waterproof matches or a lighter
- ☐ Utensils
- ☐ Forks, knives and spoons
- ☐ Manual can opener
- ☐ Tongs with long wooden handles to pick up heated containers

☐ **Special Tips:**
- ☐ If possible, store foods that do not require cooking.
- ☐ Consume foods stored in your refrigerator first. An unplugged refrigerator will remain cold for 24 hours if you don't open the door.
- ☐ Cook foods in your freezer next.
- ☐ Cook foods stored on shelves last.
- ☐ Store liquid fuels in a ventilated area such as a garage or storage shed, away from water heaters.
- ☐ Do not camp under power lines, trees or other objects that could fall or attract lightning.

☐ **Freshen Up Your Water and Food Supplies:**

Water, is essential to life, and food is also very important. Many of us could survive without food for several days. The energy, psychological comfort and nutrition that food provides are essential after experiencing disaster.

There's no assurance that food and water will be available at stores. For example, after the Northridge earthquake severely damaged the water distribution system in the city of Los Angeles, it left 100,000 homes and businesses without drinking water. Water quality was also a problem due to quake-caused interruption of the chlorination process and possible contamination through more than 2,000 pipeline breaks. People who fled their homes for nearby parks had to wait in long lines to receive food and water from the American Red Cross, Salvation Army and other volunteer agencies.

Protect your family and reduce post disaster stress by storing and refreshing your emergency water and food supplies. Some helpful hints can be found below:

☐ **Water Storage:**
Store at least a three-day to three-week supply of drinking water for each family member, (that's at least one gallon per person, per day). Water weighs 8.35 lbs per gallon and is available in juice-box type containers, cans, foil packets, plastic bottles, and long term storage containers.

- ☐ Replace your home stored drinking water every six (6) months. A 55 gallon drum will require about one cup of non-scented liquid bleach to help preserve the water during storage. Before drinking the water, open the container and let it air out.

- ☐ Store your water in a cool, dark and dry place, separated from your other emergency supplies.
- ☐ In your home store water on lower shelves, rather than on higher shelves from which containers could fall and burst.
- ☐ Store additional water for hygiene and cooking.

☐ **Alternate Water Sources:**
  - ☐ Water heater, if secured
  - ☐ Toilet Tanks (not the bowl) if the water has not been treated with chemicals to enhance color, smell, etc.
  - ☐ Beverages, try not to drink soda. Carbonation and sugar will usually make you more thirsty.
  - ☐ Ice, from your freezer, can be melted for use.
  - ☐ Swimming Pools (for hygiene purposes only, not drinkable)

☐ **Food Selection and Storage:**
  - ☐ Store non-perishable foods your family normally eats. Include items that do not require cooking.
  - ☐ Avoid foods that require a lot of water to prepare or are heavily salted. Salt will make you thirsty.
  - ☐ Remember any special dietary restrictions.
  - ☐ Be sure to keep a selection of your family's favorite treats for psychological comfort.
  - ☐ Include an emergency food supply for your pets.
  - ☐ Store at least a three-day to three-week supply of canned foods. . Foods in glass bottles and jars might break if they fall. If you decide to store these keep them secured.

- ☐ Include a manual can opener
- ☐ Open food boxes or cans carefully so you can close them tightly after each use.
- ☐ Empty open packages of flour, sugar, rice, beans, dried fruits or nuts into screw-top (plastic) jars or #10 airtight tin cans with plastic lids, to avoid problems with moisture, insects or rodents.
- ☐ Replace / renew your food supply, including canned goods, once or twice a year. Check expiration dates.
- ☐ Write the date of purchase on any new cans that you buy at the grocery store and add to you supply. Rotating your food supply is highly recommended.

Store at least a 72-hour supply of the following items:
- ☐ Charcoal, 5 gallon propane tank, lighter fluid
- ☐ Waterproof matches or a lighters
- ☐ Paper towels, plastic trash bags
- ☐ Reusable disposable eating utensils

Chapter Seven

Learn Not to Burn

Fires can put you and your home at risk, claiming the lives of thousands each year. Strong temblors can trigger fires by:

- Breaking gas lines
- Downing electrical lines
- Damaging wiring in appliances
- Toppling shelves holding combustible chemicals

Disaster-related fires are also caused by:
- Leaving food unattended on the stove after an earthquake
- Lighting or using matches before checking for gas leaks
- Using fireplaces before being inspected for damage

Having some good fire extinguishers and knowing how to properly use them before a fire occurs can save your home and your life. Please refer to the information provided below on how to operate a fire extinguisher and where to install smoke detectors.

☐ **Fire Extinguishers:**
Equip your home with dependable fire extinguishers and teach family members how to use them. Proper use of fire extinguishers can keep a small fire from growing, provide you with an escape route through a small fire and help you fight a small fire until professional firefighters arrive.

☐ **How to Operate:**

Hold the extinguisher upright and remember the word "P-A-S-S".

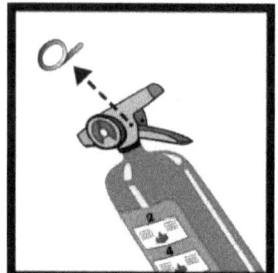

P for Pull
Pull the pin, ring or seal

A for Aim:
Aim the extinguisher nozzle at the base of the fire. Remember, most fire extinguishers last only 8-10 seconds. Make sure you aim at the base of the fire before you release.

S for Squeeze:
Squeeze or press the handle.

S for Sweep:
Sweep slowly from side to side at the base of the fire until the fire goes out.

☐ **Buying Tips:**
Several types of fire extinguishers are available.

- Extinguishers **labeled "A"** are effective for combating fires involving paper, cloth, wood or other ordinary combustibles.
- Extinguishers **labeled "B"** are effective for fighting fires involving gasoline, kitchen grease, paints, solvents or other flammable liquids.
- Extinguishers **labeled "C"** are effective for fighting fires involving electrical equipment, wiring and appliances.

Multi-purpose dry chemical extinguishers labeled "A-B-C" are effective for fighting most types of fires. Generally speaking, an "A-B-C" type extinguisher is recommended for home use and can be used at work or in your car.

Important: Fire Extinguishers have a standard life expectancy, so be sure to replace extinguishers every 2yrs, as recommended.

☐ **Smoke & Co2 Detectors:**
You can reduce your family's risk of fire or fume related death or injury, particularly during sleeping hours, by installing smoke and carbon monoxide (Co2) detectors, in the following locations

- ☐ Bedrooms
- ☐ Hallways and corridors between rooms
- ☐ Stairway ceilings
- ☐ Basements, attics and garages
- ☐ Living room and den

- **Safety Tips:**
    - Be sure to test your smoke detectors and Co2 detectors every six months and change batteries annually. This is also a good time to check your fire extinguishers.
    - Turn off gas only if you hear or smell a leak. If you do turn off the gas, you will need to call the gas company to restore service. Do not turn the gas back on yourself. Review our utilities section on page 23.
    - After a major earthquake, turn off your stove and unplug all appliances.
    - If you suspect a fire or know that one has started:
        - Follow the PASS fire extinguishing steps on page 58.
        - Inform someone to go for help.
        - Make sure you have a clear escape route before you attempt to put it out.
        - Stay low to avoid fumes and smoke.
        - Double check to make sure the fire is completely out.
        - Get out immediately and call 9-1-1 to notify authorities.

Section II

Emergency Preparedness At Work

Chapter Eight

Emergency Preparedness at Work

If you or someone you love travels to and from work every day, this next section will make a big difference in getting them home.

Below are two main reasons to have a disaster plan for your work and travel. **First**, most people consider work, home away from home. You may feel differently about that, but the 2010 census shows that most people spend 8-10 hours of their day at work. It's very probable that you could experience an emergency while there.

Second, the same census data shows that 69% of Americans spend 30 minutes or more traveling to work every day. If you traveled 40 miles per hour, in 30 minutes you would be 20 miles from home. If roads and highways have been damaged, you may end up walking those 20 miles back.

If you work for an organization, it is likely they have invested some resources in disaster preparedness and planning. What supplies do they provide at work? If your company has developed a plan, include a copy of it here. If you work for yourself, then you'll need to stock up at your home office.

Are you ready to camp out at the office for a day or two? Would you feel safe walking home from the office? What alternative routes could you use to get home? Overpasses may be down, thoroughfares possibly flooded, and entire neighborhoods could be in flames.

In a real emergency such as the one that recently hit Japan, you can expect to be stuck for at least 24 to 48 hours. It becomes very difficult to go anywhere after a major event. So the goal is to get as comfortable as possible where you are while you wait.

☐ **Travel Time, Destination & Evacuation Route:**
Using your favorite mapping site, print out your daily commute. Check for travel times by car, and by walking. Most sites will let you change from drive to walking with the click of the mouse. Get familiar with the areas you might have to walk through, and plan alternate routes if necessary. Use the lines below for travel notes.

_____

_____

_____

_____

_____

_____

_____

_____

☐ **Safe Spots:**

Using a page of graph paper from the back of this book, draw out and identify objects or places in or around your office or cubicle that will provide protection from falling objects, such as sturdy desks and tables, interior walls or corners. Draw these in **Green** and put the letter **S (Safe)** in the middle and circle it. You can also list the items in the section below.

_____
_____
_____
_____
_____
_____

☐ **Danger Spots:**

Using the same graph paper, identify objects or places in your office that pose a danger during a disaster or an emergency, such as windows, file cabinets, large office furniture, heavy objects like printers or copiers, break room appliances, plants and pictures. Draw these in **Red** and put the letter **D (Danger)** in the middle and circle it. You can list the items below.

_____
_____
_____
_____
_____
_____

☐ **Evacuation Routes:**
Your office should already have posted evacuation routes; it is federal regulation to do so. Look for these signs and possibly take a picture of it. Print it out then add it to this section as well. Use the lines below to briefly describe your exit route and meeting location.

_____
_____
_____
_____
_____

☐ **72 Hour Office Kit:**
Be sure to store a backpack, duffel bag or tote bag containing the following emergency supplies at work, plan ahead, you may want to make a few of these kits for additional areas like your car.

- ☐ **Bottled water:** At least a 72-hour supply (minimum one gallon per person, per day) to avoid significant loss of body fluids.
- ☐ **Nonperishable food:** Dried fruit, unsalted nuts and crackers, energy bars, etc.
- ☐ **First Aid kit and book:** To provide medical assistance to yourself, passengers, coworkers and others who may require aid.
- ☐ **Sealable plastic bags:** To dispose of trash, waste, etc.

- **Flashlights, spare batteries and bulbs:** To provide light if you need to walk home, find evacuation routes at night or if lights are out.
- **Essential medication:** At least a 72-hour supply of essential prescription medications to maintain your health and provide comfort while walking home or waiting for roads to re-open.
- **Tools:** Screwdrivers, pliers, rope, gloves, flashlight, eye protection, crowbars, etc., to help with debris removal and light search and rescue.
- **Pre-moistened towelettes:** For personal hygiene.
- **Extra clothes:** Shirts, pants, blouses, jackets, etc., that are comfortable.
- **Sturdy shoes:** To protect your feet from broken concrete, glass and other debris.
- **Manual can openers:** To open canned goods contained in your emergency food supply.
- **Sturdy work gloves:** To protect your hands from sharp objects you may attempt to lift.

Preassembled 72 hour kits can be purchased online at www.EmPrepBasics.com or at your local emergency supply store.

Section III

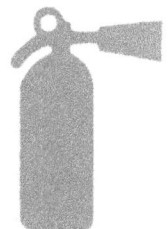

Emergency Preparedness "On The Go"

Chapter Nine

Emergency Preparedness "On The Go"

This section is geared toward helping you become aware of your surroundings. While out and about, having dinner at a restaurant or at the movies, in the mall or at a park, generally there will be people around. Given the simple nature of human beings and our inclination toward fight or flight, people tend to panic in an emergency. Becoming aware of your surroundings will help you avoid dangerous situations. The purpose of developing a mental plan of your surroundings is to help you survive while "on the go".

Where are the exits? Where will the crowd most likely gravitate? What hazards exist nearby? How do you prevent injuries when surrounded by stampeding people? What supplies do you have near you? Although you probably won't have a backpack with you while out to dinner, it will be very helpful to know that you have your emergency supplies in your car.

Remember peace of mind comes through preparation. As you develop your preparedness skills, you will soon become an expert wherever you are. What you remember about preparedness while away from home, can and will help yourself, your family and others when an emergency occurs.

☐ **Social planning:**

When out, visually take a quick inventory of exits and possible escape routes. In case of an emergency, don't rush for the doors. Stay calm. The most obvious exit isn't always the best one to go through.

    ☐ Visually take note of the exits
    ☐ Look for potential hazards nearby
    ☐ Use the stairs and avoid the use of elevators
    ☐ Remember where you parked your car
    ☐ Keep an extra pair of sturdy shoes or boots in your trunk

☐ **72 Hour Car Kit:**

This kit should include everything your office kit has. Below are the additional items you might need in your vehicle in case you're on the road when a disaster strikes. Such an event could severely damage transportation routes or cause their temporary closure.

As a result, you might have to use alternate driving routes, abandon your car and walk home or remain where you are. Store these emergency supplies in your vehicle to help make your situation less stressful.

Be sure to store these supplies in a backpack, duffel bag or tote bag. Make a new kit and include the same items as your "72 Hour Office Kit" as listed on page 66-67, and add the following items:

- ☐ **Reflectors:** To warn approaching vehicles that your car is stopped or abandoned. Check and/or replace them as needed.
- ☐ **Blanket or sleeping bag:** To provide warmth and comfort if you sleep in your car or outdoors while en route home.
- ☐ **Fire extinguisher:** To put out small fires.
- ☐ **Local maps:** To guide you if you use alternate routes to walk or drive to your destination.
- ☐ **Hat or visor:** To provide protection from the sun.
- ☐ **Whistle:** To attract attention and call for help.
- ☐ **Pen or pencil and writing pad:** for leaving messages if you abandon your car. Be sure to specify the date, time and your destination.

☐ **Hotel & Overnight Stay:**

Most hotels have an emergency plan. They often coordinate with local agencies and rely on the fire department for emergency support. In a major catastrophe, these agencies may be tied up with larger issues in throughout their community. Therefore the safety of the guests is left in the care of the hotel. Your personal preparation will make the difference.

So what can you do when you check into the hotel?

- ☐ Ask the concierge for a copy of the hotels emergency plan. This should include emergency exits, and designated meeting locations.

- ☐ Will guests be allowed to stay in the hotel after a major disaster?
- ☐ What kind of training does the hotel staff have?
- ☐ What supplies does the hotel provide, food, water, first aid?
- ☐ Check out the local area by reviewing the hotel guide book.

If you have traveled by car, make sure you have your 72 Hour Car Kit available for use. When traveling it is recommended that you bring:

- ☐ Comfortable pair of shoes
- ☐ Comfortable clothes
- ☐ Flashlight & extra batteries
- ☐ Travel first aid kit
- ☐ Have extra cash on hand, use smaller bills
- ☐ Purchase some extra water and snacks to last through your stay. Having food on hand will help, and it would also be wise to become acquainted with the local area.

Locate the nearest:

- ☐ Grocery store
- ☐ Pharmacy
- ☐ Get familiar with the area around you.

As a result, you will become better equipped to handle any emergency situation. The more you learn about your surroundings before you travel the safer your journey will be.

☐ What to do While Driving:

If you are driving when an earthquake hits, pull over to the side of the road, stop and set the parking brake. Try to avoid overpasses, bridges, power lines, signs and other hazards. Stay inside the vehicle until the shaking stops. Do not exit your vehicle if wires have fallen on it. Lastly turn on your radio for updates.

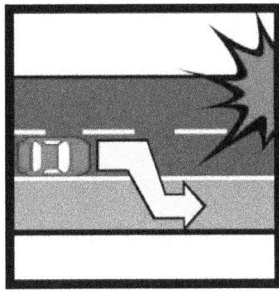

1. Use available information to evaluate the situation. If there is an explosion or other factor that makes it difficult to control the vehicle, pull over.

2. Stop the car, and set the parking brake.

3. If the emergency could impact the physical stability of the roadway, avoid overpasses, bridges, power lines, signs, and other hazards.

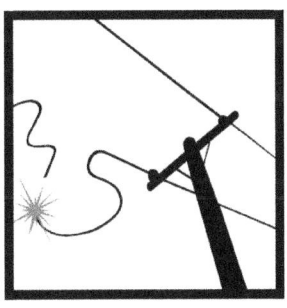

4. If a power line falls on your car you are at risk of electrical shock. Stay inside the vehicle until a trained person removes the wire.

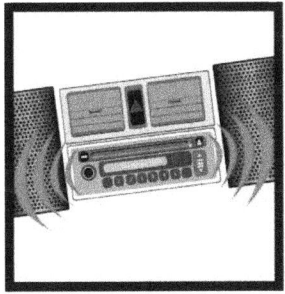

5. As with any emergency, local authorities may not immediately be able to provide information on what is happening and what you should do. However, listen to the radio for information

Conclusion

Making A Difference

Conclusion

Now that you have completed this book, you have developed your plan and gathered the resources necessary to protect and comfort your family during stressful emergency situations.

This book was created as a way to give back! It takes good people to **"*raise the flag"*** of preparedness. People like you make the difference. "How can I make a difference?" you might ask. Start by finding out what your city is doing to prepare for emergencies. Attend meeting such as city council meetings; find out if there are programs for public safety or emergency preparedness.

Most cities have programs where citizens can go for training and become involved in supporting the efforts of community emergency response teams (CERT). Your influence can and will make a difference. Share your involvement with family, friends, neighbors and coworkers. The more training you get the more valuable a resource you become.

My ultimate goal is to get you involved and interested in making you home, work, and community a safer place. The men and women who serve in the police and fire departments all over this nation will need your support during disasters. When you are able to take care of your family, you lighten their burden as well as your own.

Your well-being and safety and that of your family come first, then your neighborhood and community. There are organizations whose purpose is to support and provide help to communities in need, but they will require all the support they can get. Knowing that you have the basics will make it easier for you to support your community and their efforts to provide for those in need. Your help will support getting life back to normal as soon as possible.

I've included a list of additional web based resources that will help further your knowledge of preparation and community involvement. My challenge for you is to make a difference by getting involved, starting with yourself, your family, and your community.

Thank you for your efforts and may God bless!

Appendices

Additional Internet Resources

Please review the additional informational resources below.

www.Ready.gov: US FEMA Site for Emergency Preparedness.

www.FEMA.gov: FEMA Website includes information for many organizations (businesses, local governments, etc).

www.CitizenCorps.gov\cert\: Community Emergency Response Team, official website.

www.RedCross.org: Official Red Cross Website. Find classes, give blood, and donate to their cause.

www.DropCoverHoldOn.org: This is a fun interactive site with a game that teaches how to secure items in your home.

www.QuakeHold.com: Your best defense against earthquakes, securing furniture and other equipment.

www.ReadyAmerica.com: Additional supplies online.

www.QuakeInfo.org: How to prepare your home for an earthquake?

www.ShakeOut.org: Register for the next earthquake drill. This is a nationwide event, and one worth participating in.

www.Terremotos.org: For our Spanish speakers, very informative.

www.EarthQuakeCountry.info: Earthquake Readiness Campaign.

Please visit the following sites to purchase supplies.

www.EmPrepBasics.com Visit our website to find supplies available through our partners.

www.MorePrepared.com: Protect your world. Emergency supplies, kits, food, tools and more.

www.BePrepared.com: Emergency Essentials, disaster preparedness and more.

www.Seychelle.com: Water filtration products.

www.ProtectionAtLocation.com: PAL Kits, helping individuals at any location stay safe during man made or natural disasters.

www.DailyBread.com : Food storage with a great variety of meals to choose from.

Preparedness Gift List

Show you care! Are you having trouble deciding what to get a family member, friend or co-worker for the holidays or an upcoming birthday? If so, a survival gift might be the answer, especially for someone who has not already bought or assembled their own emergency preparedness kit. Flashlights, portable battery-operated radios, first aid kits and other emergency supplies will be valuable after a damaging earthquake since people living in the affected area might have to rely on themselves for at least 72 hours.

Make a list below of people for whom you are going to buy or assemble survival gifts.

_____
_____
_____
_____
_____
_____
_____
_____
_____

List what you think everyone needs. Depending on your financial situation and the needs of the people on your list, you might get one item or an entire kit. You can also coordinate with other relatives, friends and co-workers to buy different emergency supply items or to assemble kits as a group project, with each participant contributing one item to the kits.

The list below offers suggestions for holiday gifts that will help prepare your family, friends and neighbors for the next earthquake or emergency.

Less Than $5
- **Bottled water:** Water storage and drinking.
- **Dust mask:** To reduce inhalation of dust particles.
- **Emergency (foil) blanket:** Reflects body heat.
- **Emergency reflectors (set of four):** To warn approaching vehicles that a car is stopped or abandoned.
- **Local maps:** To guide you if you need to use alternate routes to walk or drive to your destination.
- **Manual can opener:** To open canned goods.
- **Non-perishable food:** Dried fruit, unsalted nuts and other high-energy foods to provide nourishment and energy.
- **Safety light sticks:** To provide light, especially good for use by children. Last up to 12 hours.
- **Whistle:** To signal, attract or call for help in an emergency
- **Roll of Duct Tape**: To repair bags, or use to leave notes on cars, etc.

$5 to $10

- **Emergency Preparedness Basics**: This book, written by Eric Baird available at www.EmPrepBasics.com.
- **Children's books, games, toys:** To provide comfort to children after an emergency.
- **Comfort and personal hygiene kit:** Mouthwash, toothbrush, toothpaste, wet wipes, deodorant, sunscreen, etc.
- **Flashlights, spare bulbs, and batteries:** To provide light if power is out or the user needs to walk home at night.
- **Pocket knife:** To cut rope or other materials.
- **Sturdy work gloves:** To protect hands from sharp objects and debris.

$10 to $20

- **Duffel bag or backpack:** To store items that comprise an emergency kit.
- **First aid kit and book:** To treat cuts, burns and abrasions.
- **Hand tools:** Wrenches, crowbars, pliers, screwdrivers, etc., to help turn off utilities, remove debris, etc.
- **Multi-purpose ABC-type fire extinguisher:** To help combat small residential fires that might result from downed power lines, damaged wiring in appliances or other causes (since firefighters might not be available for at least 72 hours).

- **Portable battery-operated or crank radios:** To provide access to broadcast information and instructions if power is disrupted.

Over $20
- **PAL Kits:** Located at www.ProtectionAtLocation.com. These kits include a hardhat filled with emergency supplies such as gloves, lighting and more.
- **Camp stove or barbecue:** To facilitate outdoor cooking should gas leaks or other factors making cooking indoors impractical.
- **Commercially made emergency kit:** For home, office or car. Visit our website online for additional resources.
- **Lantern:** To provide emergency lighting that does not rely on an open flame.
- **Sleeping bag:** To provide warmth and comfort if you have to sleep outside.
- **Sturdy shoes:** To protect feet from broken glass and other sharp objects.
- **Tent:** To provide protection from rain, wind and other environmental elements.

Room:

Safe Spots:

Danger Spots:

Evacuation Route:

Utilities:

Emergency Supplies in this Area:

Safe = S, Danger = D, Utilities = U, Evacuation Routes = E, Meeting Place = X

Room:

Safe Spots:

Danger Spots:

Evacuation Route:

Utilities:

Emergency Supplies in this Area:

Safe = S, Danger = D, Utilities = U, Evacuation Routes = E, Meeting Place = X

Room:

Safe Spots:

Danger Spots:

Evacuation Route:

Utilities:

Emergency Supplies in this Area:

Safe = S, Danger = D, Utilities = U, Evacuation Routes = E, Meeting Place = X

Room:

Safe Spots:

Danger Spots:

Evacuation Route:

Utilities:

Emergency Supplies in this Area:

Safe = S, Danger = D, Utilities = U, Evacuation Routes = E, Meeting Place = X

Quick Reference:
Complete this form and add it to your Emergency Kits.

Name:
SS#:
Auto Insurance Policy #:
Home Insurance Policy #:
Health Insurance Policy #:
Company:
Phone:

Family Members		
Name	**SS#**	**Phone #**

Quick Reference:
Complete this form and add it to your Emergency Kits.

Name:
SS#:
Auto Insurance Policy #:
Home Insurance Policy #:
Health Insurance Policy #:
Company:
Phone:

Family Members

Name	SS#	Phone #

Removable Checklist

Place this on your refrigerator or somewhere visible as a reminder.

Emergency Preparedness Basics Checklist

Emergency Preparedness At Home
- ☐ Safe Spots
- ☐ Danger Spots
- ☐ Evacuation Routes
- ☐ Utility Shut-Offs
- ☐ Duck Cover and Hold On
- ☐ Specific Personal Items
- ☐ Pet Preparation
- ☐ Meeting Plans
- ☐ Schools and Day-Care Center Policies
- ☐ Get to know your neighbors
- ☐ Learn What Causes Earth Quakes/Hurricanes
- ☐ Discuss Aftershocks
- ☐ Kitchen Safety
- ☐ Assemble Your Child's Emergency Kit
- ☐ Living Without Electricity
- ☐ Behavioral Changes

Supply Storage
- ☐ Supply Storage
- ☐ Food Storage

Emergency Lighting
- ☐ Flashlights
- ☐ Light Sticks
- ☐ Emergency Lighting
- ☐ Radios
- ☐ Special Power Needs
- ☐ Checking Utilities

Emergency Cash and Important Documents
- ☐ Have a Cash Stash
- ☐ Pocket Change
- ☐ Important Documents
- ☐ Storage Tips

First Aid Training and Supplies
- ☐ Common Injuries
- ☐ First Aid Courses
- ☐ First Aid Kits

Emergency Camping Out
- ☐ Outdoor Living
- ☐ Outdoor Cooking
- ☐ Cooking Supplies
- ☐ Special Tips
- ☐ Freshen Up Your Water and Food Supplies
- ☐ Water Storage
- ☐ Alternate Water Sources
- ☐ Food Selection and Storage

Learn Not to Burn
- ☐ Fire Extinguishers
- ☐ How to Operate
- ☐ Buying Tips
- ☐ Smoke & Co2 Detectors
- ☐ Safety Tips

Emergency Preparedness At Work
- ☐ Travel Time, Destination & Evacuation Route
- ☐ Safe Spots
- ☐ Danger Spots
- ☐ Evacuation Routes
- ☐ 72 Hour Office Kit

Emergency Preparedness "On The Go"
- ☐ Social planning
- ☐ 72 Hour Car Kit
- ☐ Hotel & Overnight Stay
- ☐ What to do While Driving

About the Author

Eric Paul Baird, Author of "**Emergency Preparedness Basics - *Peace of Mind Through Preparation*"**.

Eric was born in Salt Lake City, Utah, and raised in Redondo Beach, California.

While living in the beach cities of Southern California, Eric achieved the rank of "Eagle Scout" in the Boy Scouts of America, and valued the principals of the Scout Law. Motivated to succeed, Eric graduated from Mira Costa High School and later served a two year mission to Mexico, where he immersed himself in the Spanish culture.

Eric received a Bachelor's degree in Business Administration from the David Eccles School of Business at the University of Utah.

A few years later, he aspired to greater educational goals and achieved his Masters in Organizational Leadership graduating from Chapman University.

Eric values the opportunity to give back to his community by promoting emergency preparedness. He's an independent business owner. He's served on the City of Redondo Beach Public Safety Commission, advising the city council and working with police and fire departments in support of public safety and emergency preparedness programs. He's also a certified member of the Community Emergency Response Team (CERT), and values being prepared.

Eric stays busy working for a Non-profit charitable organization raising philanthropic donations supporting education and humanitarian aid efforts worldwide.

www.ingramcontent.com/pod-product-compliance
Lightning Source LLC
Chambersburg PA
CBHW060358050426
42449CB00009B/1802